By Betsy Sterman
Illustrated by Tom Mosser

CELEBRATION PRESS
Pearson Learning Group

Contents

PART 1
The Farm, 1760

"We're moving to a FARM?" I screeched. "No!"

"Lavinia Hodge, mind your manners," Mother said sharply. "I will not tolerate such unladylike behavior."

"Neither will cows and pigs," my brother George whispered in my ear. "Practice your finest curtsy for them, Mistress Vinnie!"

I squirmed away. "Why must we leave Boston?" I wailed.

Mother's face grew tight. "Your father's shipping business has failed," she said. "Four of his largest ships have gone down in storms, and his bankers will not allow him to borrow more money."

I stared. All during the winter I had heard people talking about disasters at sea. I had seen Father's growing agitation when one of his ships was overdue in port, but it had meant little to me. Here in Boston, where ships sat at wharves like huge wooden castles, the vast ocean seemed far away. A storm at sea? Why, that sounded no more dangerous than the late winter rainfall last week that had dampened my cloak.

"Your uncle Ethan is moving his family west," Mother went on. "He has left the family farm for us to live on."

"But . . ." I closed my mouth. How could the distress of a twelve-year-old girl change grown people's plans?

"Is there a house there?" I asked in a small voice.

Mother managed a smile. "A house, yes. We shall not have to sleep in the barn."

"I wouldn't mind," George put in. "Think what fun it will be to live on a farm, Vinnie!"

I glared at him. *Yes, you'd think it jolly to run about with mud on your shoes,* I thought. *But what about me? 'Tis Boston that I love.*

Oh, the narrow crooked streets, the shop windows full of laces and silks and books with fine leather bindings! People bustling about on the streets! Ships filling the harbor! Often, George and I went down to the wharf with Father to watch one of his ships being unloaded.

The big ship would sit low in the water, its masts pointing to the sky, and I could imagine its hold filled with elegant furniture from England and bundles of shimmering brocade fabric from France. Sometimes the crew bent their backs under printing presses and boxes of lead type, and once they rolled an elegant carriage with red painted wheels down the wooden gangplank and set it on the wharf to one side.

"Vinnie, look!" George had called, and I had turned from staring at the carriage to see two sailors leading a pair of fine horses off the ship. As they passed close, I shrank back. George jeered at me and called me "fainthearted," but I don't much like horses. These two, with their startled eyes and nervous twitches, had given me a special fright.

Father hasn't taken us to the wharf in a long time, I suddenly realized. Four ships, Mother had said. I tried to picture them tossing about in a howling wind, breaking into pieces under gigantic waves, and finally sinking. It was a terrible thing to lose a ship, but to lose so many, and Father's whole business with them, was beyond imagining.

I was sorry that cargo had been lost and sad for the dead seamen. What I felt worst about, though, was that with each wrecked ship a piece of my own comfortable life in Boston had been carried to the bottom of the sea.

A sob caught in my throat, and before I knew it, I had run out of the room.

"Lavinia!" Mother called, but I paid no mind. I flung open the outer door and dashed into the street toward my friend Sophie's house. Tears flooded my eyes as I ran, and I didn't see the horse until it was upon me.

It reared up, startled, eyes wild, yellow teeth biting the air as its front legs thrashed above my head. My scream must have been as loud as the horse's.

"Watch out there, missy!" a man's angry voice shouted, and through my tears and panic, I saw a man in the saddle struggling to control the animal.

The horse was so close that I could feel its heat and smell its sweat. It reared and plunged. Its hoofs clawed the air, then struck sparks on the cobblestones as they came down near my shoes. A brown flank brushed against me and flung me across the narrow street, where I slammed against the wall of a house.

Then, suddenly, horse and rider were gone, and the street was quiet again. It took me a long while to catch my breath. I could feel my heart leaping in my chest, and my whole body trembled.

I hate horses! I gasped to myself. *I hate cows and pigs and whatever else lives on a farm. I shall hate living there . . . hate it forever!*

Dear, dear Sophie,

How I miss you. The farm is as hateful as I knew it would be. The house is cramped and unbeautiful, with rough wooden floorboards. Mother says there is no point in putting down our lovely Persian carpets, so now we clatter about on bare, splintery wood.

We all try to be cheerful, but it is hard. Father grew up on this farm, and he says the soil was always thin and rocky. The fields are ready for planting, but I think our biggest crop is stones. Aunt Meg left us her kitchen garden and an onion patch, but they are both overgrown with weeds, and Mother says it is my chore to clear them.

Oh, Sophie, how unfair things are. George already has a friend! The very day we arrived, a boy of about his age appeared from the farm next to ours. He is as odious as his name, which is Putnam Bracker. Right in front of Mother and Father, he had the nerve to say how his father owns so much land hereabouts that everything will someday be called Brackerstown. Imagine! I was glad when George spoke up and said that Brackerstown was nonsense, as our own acres also reach far and even include a stream.

I have much to tell you, but paper is scarce. I think of you often. Goodbye for now, my friend, from your dear
Vinnie

Each day I watched Father trying to become a farmer again. I wondered if he yearned after his fleet of ships, but I dared not ask him. Mother, I knew, missed life in Boston, but she bent herself to the tasks of a farming woman with such good grace that I felt ashamed to bewail my own lot.

How can Mother be so uncomplaining, I wondered. *And why can't I be the same?*

Then one day I found her crying. She cried in great, muffled sobs, her apron pressed against her face as if she were spilling all the past weeks' misery into the crumpled cloth. I ran to her and we cried together, stopping only when we heard Father and George come toward the house from the barn. Mother quickly mopped her face and then my own and gave me a smile.

"Things will be better," she said.

I couldn't smile back. *No, they won't*, I thought. *Not ever.*

Strangely enough, two wonderful things happened. The first was the arrival of our hired girl. Her name was Sairy, and she had grown up on a farm. She easily did all the tasks that Mother and I struggled with.

Mistress Bracker found Sairy for us. She said, "You are doing a kindness by taking Sairy in. Her family died when their house burned down, and she has nowhere else to live."

Sairy was old, at least eighteen. Mother said that one day Sairy would likely go off to marry; but meanwhile, she relieved us of so much work that we blessed every day she was with us.

I supposed we should bless Mistress Bracker, too, but I couldn't forget that she was mother to the horrid Putnam. He persisted in boasting and was luring George into similar ways.

Sairy wanted to teach me how to milk our new cow, but I refused to go anywhere near the beast— or near Father's horse, which didn't seem to like farming any more than I did. It reared and bucked so much under the plow harness that I was perfectly content to stay far away.

I discovered the second wonderful thing by accident. One day while searching for watercress near the stream beyond the pasture, I stumbled into

9

a tangle of thorn bushes. When I managed to get free, I ran to the stream and let the swift-running water cool my bleeding hands. It was then that I heard a strange rumbling noise. Being curious, I followed the sound along the bank of the stream, until . . . oh, what a sight! There, spilling over rocks and rushing toward the stream below, was a waterfall! It tumbled and sprayed drops of water that caught the sun like tiny rainbows.

What other marvels are here? I wondered. I picked my way along the rocks at the side of the stream, and not far from the waterfall I found an old wooden bridge that spanned the stream. Eager as I was to explore the woods on the other side, I decided that some of the planks looked unsafe. So I raced home.

Father and George were just coming in when I dashed up with my questions. "Did you know we have a waterfall?" I gasped. "Does it have a name? And who built the bridge! What is on the other side?"

Father gave no sign that he had heard me. "Your father is tired, Lavinia," Mother said gently.

"So are we all, Mistress Curiosity," George said. "Tired of your questions!"

I made a face at George and pretended not to see the one that he made back at me.

I poured out my heart in a letter to Sophie.

. . . Oh, Sophie, since then I have discovered many more wonders on our farm. There are apple trees bursting with pink and white blossoms, and wildflowers growing beside the stream, yellow and pink and a shade of lavender near to that of your best silk dress. I never dreamed that spring could be so beautiful or that this place could be so filled with things to wonder about. I wish I knew more about the cavelike opening in the rocks behind the waterfall. 'Tis quite hidden by the froth of the falls. Is it a hidy-hole for an animal family? Might there be some sort of treasure hidden there? 'Tis hard to keep my curiosity in check! I'll write more later, dear friend.

One day a peddler arrived with goods on his back. Mother said we needed a sweeping broom, so he sat down and started to make one out of straw and a sapling pole. I went close and watched. I guess I asked a lot of questions, for he looked up and said, "Well, aren't you a Mistress Curiosity!"

That was George's very name for me! I felt my face redden, but then I forgot my own discomfort, for Mother laughed. It was a sound I hadn't heard since we came here. Heaven knows there was precious little to laugh about with all of us working so hard. I wished the peddler would come again soon.

11

Spring settled into summer with hot, steamy days and dark clouds that promised rain but sent none. The pasture grass turned brown. I was kept busy carrying water from the well to the wooden trough Father and George had built for the horse and cow. I was careful to stay away from both beasts, though they seemed to lack the energy to flick off a fly.

Finally, one evening, thunder rumbled across the hills and the clouds opened wide. It rained all night and all the next day and night, as if someone had taken a scissors to the clouds and cut them open. I felt snug inside the farmhouse with Father and Mother and Sairy and yes, even George.

The next morning dawned clear, but the fields were too muddy to tend. Farmer and Mistress Bracker came by in their wagon and invited Father and Mother to go visiting beyond the hills. To my dismay, Putnam Bracker jumped down from the wagon and ran for George. I retreated into the house. *Let them slosh around in the mud like a pair of oafs*, I thought. *I shall spend the day snug indoors*. I planned to braid woolen strips for a rug and take care of Sairy, who had wrenched her arm lifting a heavy kettle.

"Let's go fishing!" I heard Putnam shout. Next I knew he was bragging to us, "Get out your biggest kettle, for we'll be bringing fish enough for the whole countryside!"

"We'll catch enough for all of Boston!" George bragged, sounding like a boasting Bracker himself. I had stopped envying him his friend.

Sairy frowned. "Mind the stream," she warned. "'Tis likely swollen from so much rain."

Putnam gave a snorting laugh and off they ran. *Serves them right if they fall in and get wet*, I thought.

Hours went by, and I began to wonder why the boys didn't appear with the promised fish. Had they caught nothing and were ashamed to come back empty-handed? What if they had caught their fill and then had waded through the waterfall to explore the hollow in the rocks? What had they found there? My curiosity pinched me so hard that I bid Sairy a hasty farewell, tucked up my skirts, and ran through the muddy fields to the stream.

The water was rushing along in torrents! It was brown with mud and full of uprooted bushes, saplings, and scraps of bark. I saw no boys there with fishing lines, no baskets of freshly caught fish lying on the muddy banks. I ran upstream to the waterfall. Sheets of water plunged down over the rocks, thundering louder than ever.

"George!" I shouted. "Where are you?"

The spray flung my voice back at me. A wooden plank went tumbling crazily over the falls, and I shuddered. The bridge! Could they have been so foolish as to fish from there? A thousand "what ifs?" crowded into my head as I ran toward the bridge.

When I came to the bridge, my heart fairly leaped into my throat. Part of it was down, dangling above the torrent. Putnam knelt near the break, holding on to George, who stood perilously close to the water among the splintered boards. The broken bridge swayed above the water, putting George in danger of being swept away.

"Vinnie!" I heard Putnam shout. "George is caught! I can't get him loose! I think he is hurt!"

Sure enough, George was caught between two planks that held him fast no matter how hard he and Putnam pulled at them.

"I'll get a rope!" I shouted. Yet, I knew as I said it that I lacked the strength to pull George out.

Then I knew what I had to do. Fear surged through me, colder than the rushing water, and I stood frozen. *No, I can never do that!*

You must, I told myself.

So . . . I did.

I whirled around and ran. It seemed like miles, but at last I reached the barn. I pulled a long coil of rope down from a peg and ran into the muddy pasture, straight toward the horse.

Did I struggle more with him or more with my own fear? I don't remember. All I know is that somehow I managed to get the rope around his neck and tie a clumsy but firm knot. The animal must have felt my fear as I led him out of the pasture, for he flinched and fought, but I tried to talk soothingly as I had heard George do. When my voice quavered too much for speaking, I sang songs I remembered from my nursery years. *Oh, let him not bolt away from me*, I thought.

At last we came out of the trees and found the stream. The sight and sound of the rushing water gave the poor horse even more fright, but my own fears calmed when I saw that George had not been swept away.

I tossed the end of the rope to Putnam, but it went high and I had to pull it back. I tossed it again and again, until finally he was able to catch it. He tied it to one of the planks that had George trapped.

"Pull!" Putnam shouted. I managed to turn the horse around, so his back was to the stream, and urged him to move forward. He skittered to the side, though, and the rope lay slack.

My heart pounded loud enough to cover the sound of the water as I realized there was only one thing to do. I climbed onto a nearby stump, hoisted my skirts, and slid onto the horse's back.

"Now go!" I shouted and dug my heels into the horse's sides.

The beast lurched forward. "Pull hard!" I shouted right into his ear. The horse strained forward again, and this time I heard the crack of splintering wood behind me.

"He's free!" Putnam shouted. "Hold steady!"

I dug my hands deep into the horse's mane and pulled hard to steady him. "'Tis a good job you're doing," I said into his ear, and wondered if he would say the same to me if he had words.

Putnam and George used the rope to guide themselves to shore. I would have laughed at their bedraggled state if they were not so wet and muddy and frightened. As they sprawled in the grass, gasping, they could scarcely meet my eyes.

Finally, I slid off the horse and patted his flank. "Good fellow," I said, but I hoped he had no notion that I would ever be so close to him again.

Mother and Father came home to find George and Putnam wrapped in quilts in front of the hearth fire. Sairy and I had set their clothes in front of the fire to dry and bound George's scraped leg in a clean cloth.

The Brackers took Putnam home. I hoped they would not believe the tale he had already spun about how he alone had rescued George from foolish behavior. I saw George give him a sour look and guessed that before long his great admiration for this braggart would fade. Then George told Mother and Father what had really happened. He left out only one thing; and now that he was safe, I could not resist the chance to tease him.

"'Tis curious I am," I said in a serious voice. "Where are all the fish that you and Putnam caught?"

A bit of color came into George's face. "Oh, Vinnie, must you be so curious about everything?" he said.

"For certain you are Mistress Curiosity."

"Thankfully so," sighed Mother, and I saw Father smile. It was the first time I had seen him smile since we had left Boston.

"Curiosity is a fine virtue," he said. "Vinnie, we will name the waterfall after you. From now on, it shall be known as Curiosity Falls."

Mother smiled too. "You'll be wanting to tell Sophie about all of this," she said. "I shall take some pages out of my account book for you to write on."

I knew, of course, just what I would write.

. . . Oh, Sophie, how wonderful it is to live here at Curiosity Falls!

PART 2
The Mill, 1853

"Hurry! Get those wagons unloaded before the drivers come back!" called Mr. Greene.

Jem nodded to the owner of the paper mill. They both knew how important it was for Jem and his father to be gone from sight quickly. Jem pulled another bale of linen rags off one of the wagons, hoisted it in his arms, and hurried into the mill. Behind him, his father, slow-footed and bent, struggled with a similar load.

Even if we're not caught, we'll be at this the rest of our lives, he thought as he looked at Pa. *Up at sunrise*, he told himself as if it were an order. *Gulp down a bowl of mush. . . . Then wait for the rag wagons to come. . . . Watch out, both of you, as you peer out into the wagon yard to make sure no slave hunters are*

lurking around. . . . Then run out, unload the wagons, and carry the rags into the mill.

That was the dangerous part. Once inside the mill, they would dump the rags into vats and pound them into pulp. Then they would add water to make a wet mix, called slurry; pour the whole wet mess into the dipping trough; fetch another batch of rags; and do it all again and again. The routine was the same as yesterday—as predictable as the turning waterwheel that delivered water for the slurry.

"It's better than being a field hand," Pa would say. "Better than having your back stung with a whip if you don't pick the man's cotton fast enough."

Down in the South the man owned you, like he owned his fields and his horses and his dogs. He owned the dirt-floored cabin you lived in and the shoes on your feet and the kettle your ma cooked in. From the day you were born until the day you died, you were the man's property, and he could do what he pleased with you. *Pa's right*, Jem told himself. *This is better.*

Working at the paper mill was better, too, than running away through swamps with slave-tracking dogs on your trail, feeling scared when you ran at night, scared when you hid by day, scared when you saw others get caught and dragged back in chains, and scared when you watched your ma grow so

20

weak that finally one night she just lay down under a bush and died.

"Working hard, that's no never mind to me," Pa would say. "It's enough to be free."

They weren't really free, though. Free was what you were in Canada, where the law up there said NO SLAVERY ALLOWED and where bounty hunters couldn't catch you and take you back.

"Pa, we have to get to Canada," Jem often pleaded, but Pa would only shake his head. It was as if the terrible journey north and Ma's death on the way had sucked all the spirit out of him.

"No more running," he'd say. "No more starving, and trying to guess who's a friend or who's like to turn us in. We got to stay here where we're safe, with good people, Jem. Maybe someday things will change."

Pa was wrinkled and bent, Jem noticed, and maybe sick. Sometimes Jem could hear him cough during the night. So Jem pretended they were both safe here at the paper mill. He pretended the mill owner and his family were safe, too, for even here in Curiosity Falls, Massachusetts, far away from the slave states down south, it was a crime to shelter runaways. Kind people brave enough to do it lost their property and were taken off to jail if they were caught. That was the law.

Often Jem would steal silent looks at the mill owner and his wife and daughter, Hannah. Hannah was just a few years older than Jem.

"Keeping us here is dangerous for you folks," he had said to her once, but she had just smiled.

"We've kept others," she'd said.

You sent them on to Canada, Jem thought. None of the others had a pa holding them back. Jem wouldn't go without him. It wasn't as if he and Pa owned each other like the man had owned them, but they were family. They belonged together.

Every night while Pa slept, Jem lay beside him in the hidden room, staring up at the rough ceiling boards. Somewhere up in the sky that he couldn't see, was the North Star that had guided them to this place. It would guide them to Canada, too, if only Pa would go. *Maybe someday*, he told himself, dreaming a wide-awake dream of being truly free.

In the meantime, he and Pa made paper. The paper made at Ezra Greene's mill was sold for almanacs, books, business ledgers, wrapping paper, and writing paper.

Hannah liked to watch the papermaking. "Fancy that!" she would say. "Cloth today will be paper tomorrow and books not long after that!"

Once, as Jem pounded the rags in the big wooden vats, she pointed to the pounder in Jem's hand.

"That's a pestle," she said. "We say it 'pessel' but spell it p-e-s-t-l-e."

Hannah had explained to Jem what spelling and reading were by writing black marks on a scrap of paper, but he hadn't paid much attention.

"Words are what folks say out of their mouths," he'd said. "I don't care about marks on paper."

"Reading is important," Hannah had insisted. "Someday . . ."

"Someday I'll be free in Canada," Jem told her. "What use'll be reading to me when I'm hauling loads up there same as I do here?"

Hannah had looked at him sadly. "You just don't understand," she had said. "There are different ways to be free. Being able to read is one of them."

Jem shook his head. It didn't make sense. Still, to please her, he learned a few letters and watched while she made them into words: *Jem, mill, man, paper.*

One morning the sound of a horse cart sent Jem and Pa dashing into the secret room. Jem held his breath, then relaxed when he heard the familiar voices of a man and a young boy. Jonas Preston often brought his young son Ben with him when he came to the mill to buy paper for his print shop.

The boy jumped down from the cart and ran into the vat room. "Morning, Tom. Howdy, William!" he called to the two apprentices who stood at the dipping trough. They smiled at him but kept to the regular movements of their hands. Dip—shake—drain. Dip—shake—drain. It was important to keep the pace, drawing the wooden framed screens evenly through the liquid pulp to form layer after layer into smooth sheets of paper.

"Where's Jem?" Ben asked.

No one answered. Weeks ago, when Ben had first caught sight of Jem and his father at work in the vat room, he had asked a flurry of questions. The mill owner had taken a deep breath and drawn Ben aside.

"They are runaway slaves," he explained. "I found them in the woods one morning, near dead from hunger. They're going to stay here and work for me until I can find a way to send them on to Canada."

"Runaway slaves!" Ben had breathed.

"It's a secret, Ben," his father had said. "The biggest secret a seven-year-old boy could ever have."

Mr. Greene had nodded. "You mustn't let it slip out of your mouth into the ears of anyone else," he said, "not even your best friends."

"Oh, I won't, sir," Ben had promised, "or any grown-ups either."

Ben's father and the mill owner had exchanged uneasy glances over Ben's head. "Especially grown-ups," Mr. Greene said. Slave hunters offered to pay for information. There were some in the town of Curiosity Falls who might accept such an offer.

The men had agreed not to tell Ben about the hidden room. "It's too much to put on a boy," his father had said.

Mr. Greene and his apprentices had agreed. Tom and William were careful always to keep the drying lines full. That way, rows of finished paper hid the secret door. Even Ben, who liked to wander about and watch the papermaking, had never come upon the hidden room.

Now Ben asked again, "Where's Jem? Hasn't anyone seen him?" Jem and Pa were silent and still inside the secret room.

"Look down near the waterfall," Tom said over his shoulder as he hung another sheet of freshly dipped paper on the drying line. When Ben ran out to the stream, Tom tapped the secret code on the door. Two taps, pause. Two taps, pause. One last tap. Jem and

his father slipped out and began carrying bundles
of finished paper out to the printer's cart.

Ben returned from his search outdoors. "Jem!"
Ben shouted. "Where've you been?"

Jem smiled at the boy. "Give me some help, will
you?" As he worked, he listened to Mr. Greene and
Mr. Preston talk.

"Ezra, I'm going to need much more paper for
the print shop from now on," Mr. Preston said.
"The village is growing, and I've decided it needs a
newspaper. Can you supply me with enough cheap
paper to print a weekly news journal?"

Mr. Greene looked thoughtful. "I believe I can,
Jonas," he said. "I'll find some new rag suppliers."
He glanced over at Jem. "That means more wagons
and drivers coming in here," he said. "More chance
of Jem and his pa being seen."

The two men were silent. Then Jonas Preston walked over to Jem. "How would you like to work for me in the print shop, Jem?" he asked. "You could learn to work the press, maybe learn to set type."

To Jem's startled look he quickly added, "I've got a cellar where you could sleep. Nobody would think to search you out down there."

"And I'd keep watch!" Ben said.

Hannah, who had come up with bread and cheese for the workers' lunch, broke in excitedly. "Oh, Jem, do go to work for Mr. Preston. You'd be around words all day. What a fine chance to learn to read!"

Jem stared at the ground. "I'd be no use around words," he said. "Best I stay here with Pa."

Hannah bit her lip and turned to the printer. "Be sure to bring us copies of your newspaper, Mr. Preston," she said. "I'm going to teach Jem to read."

"Hope you have more success than my wife has had with young Ben," the printer said, smiling. "Imagine the son of a printer so lazy about words!"

"I'd rather be out here grinding pulp," Ben said. "And watching the waterwheel go 'round near the waterfall. You're so lucky, Jem."

There was an awkward silence. *Lucky?* Jem thought. *Yes, I'm lucky to have found these kind people, but all of us are in danger every day. We've got to light out for Canada, Pa. We've just got to.*

Jem tried to be busy whenever Hannah came around so she wouldn't press him to learn another letter. Once she brought a small book with her and showed it to him as he ate his morning mush. Many of the pages were blank.

"It's my journal," she said.

When Jem stared, puzzled, she explained. "I write down things that happen here each day."

"You tell about hiding Pa and me?" Jem asked, startled. "What if somebody finds it!"

"Don't fret," she said with a smile. "I keep it where nobody will ever know. You're not the only one around here with a secret place!"

It was a beautiful book. Its pages were made of her father's finest linen paper, and in the center of its brown leather cover was a large curving design.

"That's my monogram," Hannah said. Then, seeing that Jem didn't understand, she explained. "It's the first letter of each of my names, Hannah Louisa Greene. The G is in the middle, because it's the most important letter. Inside you can see I've written my whole name."

She showed Jem the flyleaf. It read:

Hannah Louisa Greene
Her Journal, 1853

Jem looked at the swirling design pressed into the leather and the fancy letters that looped and curled around each other on the page inside the book's cover. It was all so different from the plain letters she printed out for him during what she called his "lessons." *There's more to letters and words than I can ever learn*, he told himself.

In the days that followed, there was talk of strangers in the village, men looking to buy farmland nearby, or so they said.

"Don't look much like farmers to me," Jonas Preston had reported while in the mill one day.

"Slave hunters, maybe?" Mr. Greene had asked with a quick glance at Jem.

"Can't tell," the printer had answered. "I'll keep my eyes and ears open. . . ."

"I will too," Ben put in. "And my mouth closed."

The men exchanged brief smiles. So far Ben had kept his promise, but every day the danger grew.

On the Sunday that followed Mr. Preston's report of seeing strangers in town, Jem and Pa went to sit by the waterfall. Sundays were the only quiet days at the mill. There were no wagons to be unloaded, no slurry to be made, no running to the hidden room when folks from the village came to buy paper.

Every Sunday, the Greenes went off to church. Jem enjoyed the chance to spend some time alone with Pa and his own thoughts.

Today was an especially nice Sunday. The sun sparkled on the stream, swollen by a week of rain. After the damp chill of the vat room, it felt good to sit in the sun near the waterfall. The rattle of the waterwheel was loud, so Jem and his pa sat quietly without talking. Jem didn't mind.

The sound of running footsteps startled him out of his thoughts. He jumped up, hauling Pa beside him, ready to run back to the mill and into the hidden room. It was only Ben, panting and out of breath.

"Jem!" the boy gasped as he thrust a scrap of paper forward. "My pa said to show you this!"

There was writing on the paper, a few words hastily scrawled. Jem stared at it. "What is it? What's it say?"

"I don't know," Ben answered. "All I know is we were all about to go into the church when my pa heard some folks talking and he turned kind of pale. Soon as we got inside and in our seats, he tore off this piece and wrote something on it. Then he told me to make like I got a bellyache and get out of there quick and run fast as I could to show it to you. And here it is."

Jem squinted at the paper. He knew a few letters Hannah had taught him, but the words were a muddle. "Can you read?" he asked Ben urgently.

"Not so good," Ben answered. "Ma's teaching me, but . . ."

"Tell me what this says," Jem demanded. "Hurry!"

"Well . . . ." There were only four words. Slowly Ben puzzled them out. "It says . . . *sl . . . slave . . . hun-ters . . . c-com . . .* Jem! It says, *Slave hunters coming. Hide!* Oh, Jem! Slave hunters! They're coming right here! Now!"

Over the noise of the waterfall and the wheel came the sound of riders on horseback. Pa grabbed Jem's shirt.

"Let's get to the room! Quick!" he said.

"No! They'll see our footprints in the mud!" Jem shouted back. "Follow me!"

With a quick movement, Jem scrambled down the

bank of the stream, pulling Pa after him. They dodged the paddles of the waterwheel and picked their way among the rocks until they came to the bottom of the waterfall.

"Up there. Quick!" Jem said. As they clawed their way up the rocky surface of the falls, they were almost beaten back by the force of the water, but finally they hoisted themselves over a ledge into a hollow. A flurry of small brown animals leaped past them down into the stream. Jem and Pa shrank back as far as they could into the small cave, and waited.

It was hard to see through the curtain of water, but Jem saw two men on horseback ride up to Ben. They pointed at the mill and asked something, but Ben just gawked at them, hopping from one foot to another and twirling around in circles, waving a twig.

One of the men made a sign of disgust. "The boy's daft," he said. "We had better look for ourselves."

Suddenly, with a rattle of carriage wheels, Ezra Greene and his family appeared, their horse frothing as if it had been run at great speed.

"Here, now!" Jem heard the miller shout. "Who are you and what do you want?"

The strangers ignored his questions. "Queer name you folks have for this place," one of them said. "We got our own curiosity about it, ain't we, Hank?"

The second man nodded. "We're curious about if you got any runaway slaves hiding out here."

Jem pressed against the side of the hollow. "Not a one," he heard Mr. Greene say. "Don't you know it's against the law to aid runaways?"

"Sure we do," the second stranger agreed, "but folks sometimes get notions that slavery's a bad thing and the law's not worth paying mind to."

"Listen here," Mr. Greene said with anger in his voice. "I've got my own curiosities, and one of them is why you two come poking around my property looking for something that isn't here. Now get off my land, both of you. RIGHT NOW!"

As Hannah and her mother climbed down from the carriage, Ben followed the two horsemen down the road, dragging his twig aimlessly through the tall grass. Soon he came running back.

"They're gone!" Jem heard him shout.

Hannah ran into the mill, and Jem guessed she'd gone to tap the signal on the secret door. She came out with a bewildered look on her face. "They're not there," she said. "Where can they be?"

"In the falls!" Ben shouted, pointing. They all turned toward the falls, squinting and shading their eyes. At last they picked out Jem and his pa at the edge of the hollow.

"Safe!" Ezra Greene said.

"Land's sake, they're soaked to the bone!" Mrs. Greene gasped. "Hannah! Help me bring dry clothes and quilts!"

Later, after the Prestons arrived in their own carriage, everyone crowded inside the mill. As Jem told what happened, Ben stood watch at the door, but skipped back to show the piece of paper he'd stowed in his pocket.

"So, you're safe because of the words Mr. Preston wrote," Hannah said. Jem nodded, but could not meet her eyes.

"We'll have another reading lesson first thing tomorrow morning," she said firmly.

Months passed, filled with fear. Slave hunters roamed the countryside, and one day Pa said quietly, "It isn't safe here anymore, Jem. Not for us

and not for the Greenes. Time we moved on."

Jem's heart thumped. Canada! Freedom at last!

They left at the next full moon, hidden in a rag cart driven by Mr. Greene. Then it was into the forests again, sleeping by day, running at night, creeping across farm lots and edging past villages.

Once, when Jem reached deep into his pocket for the last crumbs of Mrs. Greene's bread, he found a piece of folded paper. *Good luck, Jem. I know you'll be free some day*, it said. Jem knew Hannah had written the words. He smiled. He could read most of them, especially the word *free*.

It was a peddler who, after many months, brought a letter to Hannah. She read it again and again, picturing Jem's struggle to form the words. When Ben came into the mill, Hannah grabbed him and swung him around.

"Ben, listen!" she said. She read,

"'Dear Hannah,

Pa and I are in Canada now, and we are free. I work for a printer near as nice as your pa and Mr. Preston. No more turning rags into paper. Now I turn letters into words. You were right about the ways of being free. One way is to be here. The other way is to know how to read. So I thank your family for helping us along, and I thank you for showing me this special freedom.

Tell Ben to study up on his reading. It is important. Your friend,

Jem Greene

I hope your pa won't mind that I hitched on your family name. Two names make me feel like a person who owns himself.'"

Ben clapped his hands and cried, "Hooray!"

Hannah folded the letter. *Maybe someday all slaves will be free,* she thought. *Right here in Massachusetts, not just in faraway Canada.*

After Ben left, Hannah carried a bowl of mush to the hidden door and gave the secret knock. She smiled at the young woman inside the room.

"After you eat, I'll show you the hiding place at the waterfall," she said. "And I'll tell you about letters and words."

PART 3
The Town, Present Day

The posters appeared all over town. They were in the post office, the town hall, the library, the fire and police stations, and many of the stores and businesses. Kammy pushed closer to the window of Preston's Print Shop to see what the eye-catching letters said.

"Maria, come look at this!" she called.

**MAYOR BARTON BRACKER ANNOUNCES
THE FIRST EVER**

Curiosity Falls

WACKY WHEELS RACE!
Ride your bike, trike, scooter, skateboard, skates—
ANYTHING ON WHEELS

**WHEN: Saturday, July 4, 9 A.M. to noon
WHERE: from town hall to the waterfall**

Grand Prize To The Winner!
FOOD, FUN, & A BIG SURPRISE ANNOUNCEMENT AFTER THE RACE.
SIGN-UPS AND MAPS OF RACECOURSE AVAILABLE IN TOWN HALL!

"Let's sign up!" Kammy said. "We've both got wheels." She slapped the armrest of her wheelchair.

"I don't know if my clunky old bike can get that far," Maria said.

"We'll ride together as a team," Kammy said. "Do you remember . . . ."

"Uh-oh! Kammy, look over there," Maria broke in. "It's Dan and Darcy, and they look pretty interested in the poster. They always win everything, so I guess they'll win the race, too."

Dan and Darcy Johnson were twins who were going into seventh grade next fall, like Kammy and Maria. The twins were both outstanding athletes.

"Oh, well," Maria said with a sigh. "The race is just for fun anyway. All we have to do is make it to the finish line. I wonder what the grand prize is."

"*I* wonder what the big surprise announcement

is," Kammy said. "It must be something that affects the whole town of Curiosity Falls. Anyway, I started to say, remember the story of the tortoise and the hare?"

"Sure. The hare was faster, but the tortoise won the race. So?"

"Well, in Japanese, my name—Kameko—means 'the tortoise.' I don't know how, but you and I are going to win this race, just like the tortoise!"

"July fourth is less than two weeks away," Maria said doubtfully, "but I guess we can start training for the race."

"Great idea," Kammy said. "Let's sign up at Town Hall and pick up a map. Tomorrow, we can meet at Town Hall and then practice riding the course to the waterfall."

The girls met at Town Hall the next day after lunch. "I never thought the waterfall was so far away," Kammy said after they'd ridden for a while. She pushed her wheelchair to the side of the road and gulped from her water bottle.

Maria flung herself down on the grass, out of breath. "Me either," she said. "Not that I'm tired or anything. That panting sound you hear is just Old Clunky." She pointed to her bike.

"This race is definitely going to build our muscles," Kammy said cheerfully.

"Hey, look!" Maria said suddenly. "It's the super twins!" Darcy and Dan Johnson whizzed past them on streamlined mountain bikes, bending low over the handlebars and pumping hard. Darcy's hair streamed out from under her helmet, and Dan's goggles seemed glued to his face by the wind.

"Do you still think we tortoises are going to win?" Maria asked.

Kammy grimaced. "Let's get back on the road."

Maria hauled herself back onto her bike, and they started off. The route to the waterfall led them out of the residential part of town and down a wooded lane.

"We're here!" shouted Maria at last. "Hi, Darcy. Hi, Dan."

The twins waved back. They had set their bikes down carefully and were sitting in the grass near the waterfall. Kammy pushed her way through the grass. "Wow, it's pretty here," she said.

Dan laughed. "What's pretty about a broken-down old waterwheel and a building that's falling apart?" he said. "Oh, well, it's all going to be torn down anyway."

"Torn down? Who said?" Maria asked.

"We heard Mayor Bracker telling Dad," Dan answered.

Darcy explained, "The mayor's selling all this land to a developer. The new owner is going to build

fancy houses surrounding a golf course."

"Can Mayor Bracker do that?" Kammy asked. "Is it his land?"

"He says it is," Dan answered, "but Dad is a lawyer, and he said only a deed can prove it."

"So that's what the big surprise announcement is going to be," Kammy said. She looked around at the stream, the waterfall, the woods, and the fields. "I always thought the town owned all of this."

"I guess everybody thought so," Dan said. "That's why Dad told Mayor Bracker he would need written proof that the land is his."

"I heard the Mayor say something about planting palm trees," Darcy said.

"Here? You're kidding!" Maria laughed. "How long would they last in the wintertime?"

Kammy frowned. "Hey, you guys, it isn't funny,"

she said. "Mayor Bracker can't ruin a place as historical as this. It's really special."

"It's just an old paper mill," Dan said.

"Yes, but long ago it was important to everybody in the whole valley," Kammy said. "Everyone wrote letters and kept track of their businesses on paper made right here!"

"They read newspapers printed on Curiosity Falls paper, too," Maria added. "You know Mr. Preston at the print shop? He told us it was an ancestor of his who printed the first newspaper in Curiosity Falls. This place is really special. It should be fixed up, not torn down."

"In Japan, places with a high artistic or historical value are called national treasures, and people come from all over to visit them. Why couldn't the mill be like that?" Kammy asked.

"Is it special enough, though?" Darcy asked. "After all, our state is filled with old mills. Well, if you do find a way to save the mill, count us in." She turned to Dan and said, "Race you home!"

Kammy and Maria made their way back to town. "Where would that deed be, if there was one?" Maria asked. "I'm going to visit Gran. She might have some ideas."

"I have to get to my piano lesson. See you tomorrow!" Kammy called.

Maria parked her bike near a sign that read CURIOSITY FALLS RETIREMENT COMMUNITY. Fluttering from the sign was a Wacky Wheels Race poster.

Maria pulled off the poster and made her way around to the wide stone patio. There sat Gran in her motorized wheelchair near a bed of marigolds, leaning forward to pinch off wilted flowers.

Gran looked up and gave Maria a cheery wave. "I was hoping you'd come today," she said. "What's new?"

"Lots," Maria said. "Look at this." She held up the poster and helped Gran find her reading glasses.

"Sounds like fun," Gran said. "Maybe I'll race, too. Are you and Kammy going to be in it?"

"We already signed up," Maria said. "But there's more." She told Gran what she knew about Mayor Bracker's plan.

"Tear down the old mill?" Gran sputtered. "Impossible! That mill carries the history of the town with it. This is all those Brackers' fault. They've been proud as pigs in a palace, ever since the early days of the town."

Maria laughed. "Come on, Gran, you can't know that!" she said.

"Can't I? Come with me!" Gran said.

"There!" Gran said when they were inside her apartment. "Just look at that!"

Maria stared at the large glass-covered frame on the wall. She'd never paid much attention to the old letters inside.

"These are letters that were written long ago to my great-great-great . . . oh, I don't know how many greats grandmother. Sophie was her name."

"Who wrote them?"

"Sophie's best friend, Lavinia Hodge. Vinnie lived on a farm near the waterfall."

"Near *our* waterfall? Wow!"

"Here, read this part," Gran said, pointing.

Maria edged close to the glass. "'*He is as odious as his name, which is Putnam Bracker,*'" she read. "Bracker! Is that like Mayor Bracker?"

"That's right," Gran said. "Read on."

"'Right in front of Mother and Father, he had the nerve to say how his father owns so much land hereabouts that everything will someday be called Brackerstown. Imagine! I was glad when George spoke up and said that Brackerstown was nonsense, as our own acres also reach far and even include a stream.'"

Maria thought hard. "Do you suppose the Hodge family's acres included the waterfall and the land around it?"

"Let's hope so," Gran said.

"There has to be a deed or something to show who the real owner is," Maria said. "Without that—well, you know Mayor Bracker."

"Indeed I do," Gran said. "Barton Bracker's a braggart, just like that long-ago boy Putnam."

She looked up at the letters. "These are very precious to me," she said. "I mean to give them to the Historical Society someday, but everything there is in such a muddle that I'm not in a hurry." She shook her head. "There are boxes of books and paper, nothing's in the proper order, labels are missing. You can't tell what is from the Civil War and what is from the Revolution."

Maria felt her heart jump. "Do you think maybe the deed is in one of those boxes?"

Gran's face lit up. "Let's have a look. Call Kammy, and we'll go first thing tomorrow!"

The searchers met at the historical society the next morning. The society had given them permission to look in the storage room. For hours they dug in boxes, coming up with old pictures, drawings, letters, maps, and books. They found everything but the old deed.

Kammy pushed her wheelchair into a corner of the room. "Let's look in this trunk," she said.

The trunk was easy to open, for the lock was broken. Kammy dug through carefully folded skirts, aprons, and shawls. "Old clothes," she said. "Wait a minute, here's a package, all wrapped up."

Gran and Maria watched as Kammy carefully peeled away the cloth wrappings. "It's a book," Kammy said. She ran her fingers over the leather binding. "There are letters stamped on it. H-G-L."

"That's somebody's monogram," Gran said. "Open it, Kammy."

Kammy said, "It's a diary. Look."

They stared at the first page.

*Hannah Louisa Greene
Her Journal, 1855*

"Wow!" Maria said. "That was before the Civil War. I wonder what Hannah had to write about."

Kammy looked up from her reading. "Plenty," she said. "Listen to this." She read, "'*Passengers arrived again last night. There were two this time—a boy and his father. The boy looks to be about 12 years old. Both were quite worn down, of course, so Poppa stowed them safely in the hidden room, off the vat room. I helped take down the drying paper to reveal the door. Momma and I took them bread and soup. There was no sleep for us after that. For the rest of the night we listened for sounds of tracking dogs and slave hunters, but all was quiet.*'"

"Slave hunters!" Maria breathed. "The boy and his father were runaway slaves!"

Kammy nodded excitedly. "She calls them passengers," she said, "and talks about a hidden room. Hannah Louisa Greene and her parents were running an Underground Railroad station!"

"Heard there were lots of them around this part of the country," Gran said, "but I think Hannah's journal might tell us something more, girls. Kammy, may I look at that book for a moment?"

Both girls watched as Gran turned the pages, nodding. She looked up. "It's just as I thought," she said. "The station was the old paper mill!"

Kammy touched the old book gently. "I *knew* the mill was a national treasure," she said.

"Let's go back to my apartment," Gran said. "We have some phone calls to make!"

Between training for the race and helping Gran with the project to save the mill, Kammy and Maria hardly had a chance to draw a breath in the days leading up to the Fourth of July. Dan and Darcy were training, too, but they volunteered their time once Kammy and Maria told them what was going on. The people at the Historical Society helped, too. They carefully photographed the pages of Hannah's journal, while Gran made a flurry of telephone calls.

At last, July fourth came. Kammy, Maria, Dan, and Darcy all gathered at the town hall for the big race.

"Bicycles over here! Skateboards, scooters, and skates over there!" Mayor Bracker's voice boomed over the loudspeaker at Town Hall. "Strollers, stay together till the starting whistle. Everyone listen for your instructions!"

The crowd buzzed with excitement. Dan and Darcy left their bikes and ran over. "Is he here yet?" Darcy asked.

"No," Kammy said. She scanned the crowd nervously. "But he promised he would be."

"Do you think our plan will work?" Dan said.

"Sure," Kammy said. *I hope so*, she said to herself.

The loudspeaker squawked. "Ladies and gentlemen, boys and girls," the mayor's voice boomed. "Get ready for take-off! Ten, nine, eight, seven, six, five, four, three, two, one . . . ."

Loud cheers drowned out his voice, and the Wacky Wheels Race began.

"Hey! This is fun!" Maria called as they coasted down a small rise.

Kammy grinned back. In spite of her worry, it really was fun. All around, people were laughing and calling out to each other. A man pedaling furiously on a tall unicycle passed by and waved. Young mothers pushing strollers ran past, laughing, while the children in the strollers shouted with delight.

Gran whizzed by in her motorized wheelchair. "How are you doing, Gran?" Maria called.

"Just fine!" Gran called back. "Got myself a brand-new battery!"

"Heads up, everybody," a familiar voice called. "Make way!" It was Mayor Bracker, bustling by in a golf cart decorated with tiny plastic palm trees.

"There are my mom and dad!" Maria said.

"Mine, too!" Kammy said. She rolled along breathlessly for a minute or two. "Maria," she burst out, "we haven't seen him anywhere. What if he forgot? What if he got the wrong day?"

"Stop worrying!" Maria said.

"I will if you will," Kammy replied. They grinned at each other and didn't speak again till they'd crossed the finish line.

They were far from first place. When Kammy and Maria and a few other stragglers came puffing up to the finish line, people who had already finished were sprawled on the grass or lined up for lemonade and cookies.

Darcy and Dan ran up. "We won!" Dan said excitedly.

"It was a tie, and there's only one prize, so we're going to take turns with it," Darcy said. "Look!"

She showed them a giant yellow button with crimped blue satin around the edges. Two blue satin streamers hung from the bottom. On the button was printed WACKY WHEELS RACE WINNER!

"Great going, you two!" Maria said. She winked at Kammy and added, "At least we tortoises managed to finish the race!"

"Has the mayor made his big announcement yet?" Kammy wanted to know.

"Not yet," Dan said. "They're setting up a platform for him. Don't worry, Kammy. Our plan is going to work just fine."

Kammy wasn't worried about the platform. She had a bigger worry. "Is our guest here? Please, please say he is!" she begged.

"He is!" Darcy said. "Look over there! We were just waiting for you to get here to go meet him."

A tall man in a blue summer suit stood apart from the crowd, talking to Gran. Kammy felt her breath rush out in a long sigh. Maria flung down her bicycle. She and Kammy raced over to Gran, with Dan and Darcy close behind.

"Hi!" Maria said to the man in the suit. "I'm Maria. We're sure glad you made it!"

"Thank you so much for coming!" Kammy added. "I'm Kammy and they are Darcy and Dan."

"I've heard a lot about you kids," the man said warmly, shaking everyone's hands. "You've done good work by helping Mrs. Todd."

The sound system squawked as Mayor Bracker climbed onto the wooden platform. "Can someone turn off that noisy waterfall?" he joked.

There was a spatter of laughter. The mayor

fingered the lei of flowers around his neck. "I know you're all waiting for my announcement. But first, I'd like to ask all of you to take a look around. See this broken-down, old mill and the overgrown fields? Now, imagine all of this being swept away and made into something new and modern and beautiful!"

Kammy felt Maria squeeze her arm. "I can't believe he's trying to go ahead and push his plan through without the deed," she whispered. Maria nodded. The crowd had gone silent.

"Picture it," the mayor said with a wave of his hand. "There'll be beautiful houses here, surrounding a golf course, with a fine big restaurant and even a swimming pool."

Gran spoke up. "Sounds lovely, Mayor Bracker," she said sweetly. "Of course, the golf course and pool will be open to us all?"

"Well . . . er . . . not exactly," said the mayor. "Just to the folks who buy the houses. But all of you will be welcome to enjoy the view. . . ."

Laughter and angry hoots blotted out his words. Kammy glanced at Maria, Darcy, and Dan. "This is it," she said. "Let's go." They headed for the platform.

Kammy looked up at the mayor. "Excuse me, Mayor Bracker," she said politely. "I have an announcement to make, too."

The mayor frowned down at her. "Just who are you, young lady?" he asked.

Kammy didn't answer. She took a tight grip on the armrests as Maria, Darcy, and Dan lifted her wheelchair up onto the platform beside the startled mayor. The three friends climbed up too.

"Here now!" sputtered the mayor. "You can't just barge up here and—"

"Let her talk!" someone shouted. The mayor turned red but handed Kammy the microphone.

Kammy swallowed. "My name is Kameko Mitsui," she said. "This is my friend Maria, and of course, you know Darcy and Dan, the race winners!"

The crowd cheered.

"We're all proud to live in Curiosity Falls, just like you," Kammy went on, "but until lately, we thought it was just an ordinary town. Then we found out that about a hundred and fifty years ago, Curiosity Falls had a special secret. Only a few people knew about it, but something dangerous and important was going on right here at the old paper mill."

Voices murmured and heads turned toward the mill. Kammy felt her own voice grow stronger as she described the Underground Railroad, the secret system that many people who were against slavery had set up to help runaway slaves escape to freedom.

"Let me tell you about the role that the mill played in the Underground Railroad," she said. She described Ezra Greene and his family, the mill's secret room, and the hidden cave behind the waterfall. She told about Jem and his father and Mr. Preston, the printer, and his young son Ben.

"They were all in this together," she said, "and it was the scariest thing they'd ever done in their lives."

"Well now, young lady," the mayor put in, "this is an interesting history lesson, if it's true. But I don't . . ."

"Oh, it's true, all right," Maria said. She pulled a sheaf of papers from her backpack. "This is a photocopy of Hannah Greene's journal," she said. "It's all in here."

"And guess what!" Darcy put in. "Now that the journal has been found, our own Mr. Preston is going to print copies of it." Everyone except Mayor Bracker clapped and cheered.

"Uh, yes, very interesting," he said, "but what does it have to do with our development?"

Kammy leaned forward to the crowd. "This mill is a very special place," she said. "If we choose, we can keep it special."

"How?" voices shouted.

Kammy smiled at the man in the blue suit, who was stepping up onto the platform. "This is Mr. Edward Wills," she said. "He'll tell you all about it!"

While the mayor listened open-mouthed, Mr. Wills told about the national program he represented. It helped towns find funding to rebuild sites that had been stations on the Underground Railroad. "Judging from the evidence I've seen, the paper mill in Curiosity Falls will be eligible for funding," he said. "The Historical Society has investigated the old mill and found the secret room." The crowd buzzed with excitement.

"What do you think, everyone?" Kammy said after Mr. Wills had finished speaking. "Should we rebuild the mill or put up a golf course here?"

On the spot, the town voted to preserve the mill. The only dissenting vote was Mayor Bracker's.

After the vote, people gathered in small, excited groups, talking about rebuilding the mill. There was a crowd several people deep around Mr. Wills.

"Whew!" Maria said when groups finally began

breaking up and drifting home. "What a day!"

"I never thought it would happen," Darcy said.

"I did," Kammy said quietly.

Gran chuckled. "Did you see the mayor's face when Mr. Wills was talking?" she said. "Oh, Vinnie Hodge, it took many years, but a bragging Bracker finally got what he deserved!"

Kammy sighed. "So it will all be rebuilt, just as it was in Hannah Greene's day. The vat room, the drying racks, the secret room where Jem and his father lived . . . ."

"And no palm trees to hide the cave behind the waterfall!" Darcy laughed.

The sound of a horn made them all sit up. "Here's the bus from the retirement home," Gran said. She scooted her motorized chair toward the ramp.

"Just a minute, Mrs. Todd," Dan said. "Darcy and I have something to say. She and I won the race, but, well, we think the big winner today is the whole town of Curiosity Falls."

"So the prize really belongs to Kammy and Maria," Darcy said. She held out the big yellow button. "Sorry there's only one of these. I guess you'll have to share."

Maria grinned at Kammy. "You can wear it first," she said. "It really was the tortoise who won the race, after all!"